THE
PLAYER'S
HITLIST

A
Tennis
Reference
Guide
For
Competitive
Play
by

NEIL
ADAMS

"The ultimate competitive strategy is to remain centered in your own unshakable confidence and calm, free of anyone else's influence."

The Inner Athlete
Dan Millman

FOREWORD

In a society where everyone is looking for the quick answer, there comes a need for a resource that provides that service. And tennis is no exception. How many times have I watched players at major tournaments have the look of confusion on changeovers, not knowing how to handle a cheater or beginning to choke when up 5-2 in the third?

Often in a tennis match, we find ourselves in a quandary. "I'm at the end of two long sets, readying to play the third and I'm tired. What should I eat?" Or, "my new shoes are beginning to rub my foot. What should I do *right now* to avoid a blister?" Or, "I'm playing a pusher and *I hate pushers*. What should I think about right *now*?"

Neil Adams has not gone into a long treatise of techniques, nutrition, sports medicine or psychology. He has purposely written this book for the competitor who goes through any of the concerns I just mentioned. This is the synopsis you've been looking for. Quick, succinct answers to your immediate needs. But, I caution you to be careful about one thing. It would be easy for you to have a problem during a match, read Neil Adams' recommendation and say, "Oh great, how do I do that?" Don't become analytical reading this. Neil Adams has significant experience in competition. If you trust his instruction, you'll win more than you've been winning. Remember, being a great tennis player is a long distance race; it's not a sprint.

Jack L. Groppel, Ph.D.
Executive Vice President
LGE Sport Science, Inc.
Orlando, Florida

PREFACE

THE PLAYER'S HITLIST™ works like an on court coach. As an active teaching professional, I realize I cannot always be there for every practice session and competitive match my students play. So I prepared this reference guide to assist the tennis competitor going to battle.

Because every well fought battle involves strategy, planning, training, supplies, and preparation, THE PLAYER'S HITLIST touches also on these backgrounds to victory. I am giving you concise guidelines and the book fits easily into your racquet bag. You will have at your finger tips recommendations and information that every good coach makes and knows. Notice the extra "personal note" page at the end of the appropriate sections for you to jot down your own reminders in particular situations. Incorporate these methods and thinking processes into your approach to match play, and you will be ready to fight the good fight and WIN!

I complete the book with two general guideline sections relating to mental toughness and the development of a proper training program: two areas of tennis, often neglected, that can make a difference in your success and enjoyment in competition.

Read this 'HITLIST' cover to cover to become familiar with the contents. Then, let it be your guide, your quick reference, a coaching tool, and a reminder of what you can do in specific competitive situations. You can refer back to various sections again and again as your need or your interest arises.

Good luck with your game and your matches. May 'THE PLAYER'S HITLIST' enhance your journey!

ACKNOWLEDGEMENTS

Throughout my playing, teaching, and coaching career, I have been privileged to learn from and to be supported and inspired by special people. I would like to take this opportunity to thank Arthur Jennings, Mike Ferrill, Beth Walker, Avery Rush, Don Usher, Dr. Jack Groppel, Brad Louderback, and thanks to Bob McKinley for bringing me back to the teaching that I love. I must express my love and gratitude to Jan Harris for her many hours of involvement in the writing, editing, and design of the book. Thanks to Greg and Carrie Wehmeyer for their help in finalizing this edition. I always deeply appreciate the love and support I receive from my family, Sylvia, Jerry, Wendy, and Michael.

viii

TABLE OF CONTENTS

PREPARATION

Whether in or out of town, your readiness for tournament play depends on what preparations you make as you go out to face your challengers. Maintaining your routine and getting the "little stuff" taken care of in advance prepares you to concentrate on your competitive event. Here are checklists to help you prepare.

ONE WEEK BEFORE

Confirm Housing
* Make sure of your arrangements for overnight stays.

Restring
* Consider whether your racquets need to be restrung.

Stay In Training
* Remain consistent and disciplined in your training (your eating, sleeping, & practice).

Taper Your Workouts
* Go through your usual workouts, but gradually shorten the practice time as your event approaches.

Practice Competition
* Duplicate the condition of actual competitive play in practice as often as possible.

Begin A Seven Day Routine
* Follow your 7-day pre-competition routine. Create this with your pro or coach, if you do not yet have one.

TWO DAYS BEFORE

Get Site Locations & Directions
  • Confirm locations and directions to your match site(s).
Know Your Draw
  • Find out your draw. Get a copy if you can.
Develop A Game Plan
  • Formulate your game plan for the first match.
    Collect information about your opponent. See
    Scouting Your Opponent and Creating A Game
    Plan in this book.
Check The Weather
  • Watch the extended weather forecast. Pack accordingly.
Play It In Your Head
  • Begin mentally rehearsing how you want to
    perform in this tournament.
Begin A 24-Hour Routine
  • Follow your 24-hour pre-competition routine.
    Create this with your pro or coach, if you have not
    yet done so.

PACKING YOUR ON-COURT BAG

It is good to have a small duffel bag with a few essentials
in it.
  • a fresh can of tennis balls
  • a fresh, dry shirt and pair of socks
  • sunscreen (choose an SPF 15 or higher)
  • lip balm
  • a set of string
  • an extra overgrip or replacement grip
  • a hat or visor
  • bandages and pre-moistened towelettes (for blisters)
  • a bandanna (to dip into ice water for cooling purposes)
  • wristbands
  • a towel

- an energy bar or other carbohydrate snacks
- a water jug
- a few Emergen-C™ packets for handy electrolytes (available at most health food stores, mixes with water)
- a USTA rule book
- your copy of THE PLAYER'S HITLIST™

BE PREPARED FOR ADVERSITY

These checks should prepare you for just about anything. Keep in mind, anything and everything can happen. If you allow yourself to be surprised, you will be unprepared, and the unprepared athlete is in trouble.

PERSONAL NOTES

_____

_____

_____

_____

_____

_____

_____

_____

_____

_____

_____

_____

_____

_____

_____

_____

_____

_____

_____

_____

_____

_____

BE PREPARED FOR YOUR OPPORTUNITY TO WIN!

CREATING A GAME PLAN

A Game Plan is *a planned strategy for winning.*
Why is it critical to have a game plan? With a game plan you are clear and focused on what you must do to win your match. You are not simply hitting balls and "hoping" to win. Knowing *how* you plan to win, you are less in doubt about winning. Your winning confidence eliminates your fear. A fearful player makes careless errors and can lose. With a game plan you are *planning on winning.*

Greatly increase your winning confidence by collecting and analyzing the following information. Keep it simple!

Your Game
* Define your style of play.
* Identify your strengths and weaknesses.

Your Opponent's game
* Scout or otherwise learn about your opponent.
* Identify strengths and weaknesses in the physical, mental, and emotional style of play exhibited by your opponent.

Your Court And Special Conditions
* Factor the court surface into your plan. (type and/or texture of surface)
* Consider the probable wind, heat, cold, or other factors with which you may be playing.

A solid game plan will capitalize on your opponent's weaknesses and your particular strengths and style of play.

BACKUP GAME PLAN

Have a plan B, in case plan A is not working. You might want to have three plans! Be prepared with alternatives and be flexible. Write down your strategies and keep them with you. Create a habit of seeing what is happening and responding with a strategy.

PERSONAL NOTES

_____

_____

_____

_____

_____

_____

_____

_____

_____

_____

_____

_____

_____

_____

_____

_____

_____

_____

_____

_____

_____

_____

KEEP IT SIMPLE!

SCOUTING YOUR OPPONENT

You have two opportunities to scout your opponent's style of play before you formulate a game plan to meet it. You can view a match prior to your match, or pay close attention during your match warm-up.

VIEWING A PRIOR MATCH

Your best opportunity to develop a strategy against another player is watching their match against someone else. Take notes on the following:

BASELINE STRENGTHS AND WEAKNESSES

Groundstrokes
- Do you see a considerable strength or a particular weakness from the baseline in their forehand or backhand?
- If you do not see one, watch which stroke the player prefers to hit when receiving a ball hit to the middle of the court.

Strategy: Hit balls to the side the player prefers the least, the weakness, in order to control the point.

MIDCOURT AND NET GAME

Net Game And Passing Shots
- How effective is this player's approach shot? (top spin, flat or underspin)
- How often does this player come to the net? Watch their movement. They will either hang back at the service line after their first volley or they will close into the net.

8

• Do you see a weak side in their volleys?

Strategy: Hit your passing shots as early as you comfortably can to your opponent's weak volley side in order to counter his or her aggressive move.

SERVE
Strong Serve
• Does this player serve with a lot of pace or spin?

Strategy: Move up or back a bit to adjust your return to be your most effective against the serve.

Service Pattern
• Where does the player like to put the serve?

Strategy: Position yourself in a way to close the opening he enjoys serving to.

Second Serve
• How strong is his or her 2nd serve? Look at the pace, spin, and directional control.

Strategy: Attack the 2nd serve by moving forward and hitting a strong return to the player's weak side.

STYLE OF PLAY
Game Preference
• Do you consider this player to be a 'baseliner,' an 'all courter,' or a 'serve and volleyer'?

Strategy: Take advantage of an opponent's preferred style by playing to take him out of the game he likes. For example, bring a baseliner into the net occasionally, to keep him from getting grooved at the baseline. This also keeps your opponent off balance.

FOOTWORK AND BASELINE POSITIONING

In General

- Does the player move quickly or slowly getting to balls?
- Where does the player position himself at the baseline?

Aggressive Player

- A player who stays close to the baseline and takes the ball on the rise, waist to shoulder high, has an aggressive game.
- Aggressive players prefer ending a point quickly.

Strategy: Back an aggressive player off the baseline with higher net clearance and putting your shots as deep as possible. Keep the ball in play as long as possible against these players. This should limit their aggressive game and keep you in control of the points.

Passive Player

- A player who stays farther behind the baseline, three feet or more, and lets the ball drop considerably before hitting it, about knee high, has a passive game.

Strategy:Move a passive player diagonally across the court both in front of and behind the baseline. This gives him less time to get into position to hit the ball comfortably. Bring him to the net occasionally. More secure at the baseline, this puts a passive player out of balance.

SPINS

- Does the player hit a predominant spin from either or both sides at the baseline?

- Notice the height at which she hits the spin in relation to her body: at shoulder, waist, or knee. This is her 'hitting zone.'

  Strategy: Attempt to keep the ball out of her hitting zone as much as possible.

PACE

Pace-lovers and Pushers

- Does this player hit the ball with a lot of pace?
- Does he or she hit better or when you hit with a lot of pace or just a little? Most players generally like one or the other.

  Strategy: Adjust your pace to one you can be comfortable with, and will take your opponent out of his comfort zone.

SYNTHESIZING YOUR INFORMATION

Keep Your Game Plan Simple

- Do not over-analyze your future opponent's game. You only need enough information to formulate a few basic strategies. You may have enough information after watching the player for ten or fifteen minutes. For example: information such as 'a baseliner with a weak backhand, a weak second serve, and does not come to the net' translates into a fairly simple game plan.
- Consider your own game in relation to this opponent's style.
- After you play your match, you might take other notes for future reference.

MATCH WARM-UP

If you have only your match warm-up in which to scout your opponent and quickly set up a game plan, focus on the following.

1. Strong or weak side at the baseline and net.
2. Serve
3. Spins
4. Baseline Positioning

Pick up a few of these simple pointers as you are hitting with your opponent. You should be close to 'match ready' before you go on the court. Pay attention and prepare to win.

PERSONAL NOTES

_____

_____

_____

_____

_____

_____

_____

_____

_____

_____

_____

_____

_____

_____

_____

_____

_____

_____

_____

_____

_____

_____

LOOK FOR THE IMPORTANT THINGS!

PLAYING IN ADVERSE CONDITIONS

THE WIND

Playing in windy conditions presents a challenge for most people. Here is what you do to compensate for the wind.

IN ANY STRONG WIND

Good Footwork
- Take short quick steps to the ball. Stay ready for any abrupt movement of the ball. Expect the ball to move unexpectedly.

Acclimate To Each Wind Condition
- Get out on the court before your match, if you can. Hit on each side of the court, adjusting your shots against and with the wind.

AGAINST THE WIND (Wind To Your Face)

Hit With Topspin
- The ball will *drop* more with the air pushing down on it (topspin). An underspin ball will float.

Give Yourself More Net Clearance
- More net clearance carries the ball deeper against the wind resistance.

OR: *If you do not own topspin groundstrokes, hit as flat as possible and hit the ball higher.*

14

WITH THE WIND (Wind To Your Back)

Hit An Underspin Drive
- With the wind behind it, it is the underspin drive that will make the ball drop, not topspin. Hitting topspin in this wind condition will cause the ball to float.

Shorten Your Backswing
- A more compact backswing will give you more control.

OR: *If you do not hit underspin yet, hit as flat as you can.*
- *Shorten the court lengthwise and hit as flat as possible.*
- *Shorten the court rather than lower your net clearance.*

TEMPERATURE EXTREMES:

Take Special Precautions

IN THE HEAT

Hydrate Your Body
- Proper hydration is vital. Make sure that you drink plenty of water before, during, and after your match or practice.
- Water is the best fluid replacement, but you can also take in a water diluted sports drink (a 1:1 ration).
- Water will sustain you up to 90 minutes during play. After this period, you will need carbohydrates to maintain a good energy level.

Apply Sunscreen
- Protect your skin with sunscreen (use SPF 15 or higher).

Protect Your Head And Feet
- The outer extremities of the body, the head and feet, are the most affected by the temperature.

15

- Protect your head and face with some form of headwear.
- Prevent heat-related blistering by wearing two pair of socks (or one pair of Thorlo™ socks).

Keep Cool
- Dip a rolled-up bandana into ice water and place it behind your neck on changeovers.
- You can tie an ice water-dipped bandana around your neck for more comfort during play (try it, it's refreshing).

Continue To Drink Water
- Drink at least 4 ounces of water (a couple of good sips) *every ten to fifteen minutes* regardless of when you get a changeover break.
- Drink plenty of water *between matches*.
- Drink water without waiting to be thirsty. By the time you are thirsty, you are already dehydrated.

IN THE COLD
Warm Up More
- Take extra time to raise your body temperature before you go out on the court. Do some light jogging and stretches. You should do this no matter what the weather, but take some extra time in the cold.

Wear Layers
- Since your body will gradually warm up, you should dress accordingly. Wear a few thin layers. As you warm up and perspire, remove layers as needed.

Drink Water
- Although you may not be perspiring much, especially in dry climates, do not be fooled. You can become

dehydrated in the cold.
- Continue to drink water on changeovers.

Cool Down Slowly
- Directly following a match or practice, put dry layers of clothing back on. Wearing layers now will allow your warm body to cool down gradually.

DELAYS

Your routine for handling a delay should be whatever will work for you, in particular. Ask yourself these questions when deciding how you can best manage your delays.

Consider Factors
- How much time do you have? Contact the tournament desk to know your time frame, then set up your routine.
- Do you need to refuel? See Fueling Yourself For Competition.
- If you are in the middle of a match, do you need to talk strategy with your coach? Take notes and study them before going back out on the court.

Your Personality
- Does music help you to relax? If so, take your player and headphones and listen to some.
- Do you become "stale" by hanging around? Leave the facility if you need to. Consider how much time you will need to refocus on your match when you return.
- How are you going to refocus your attention on your match when the delay is over?
- What is your arousal level? Take whatever steps necessary to get to an ideal state. Refer to Managing Arousal Levels, and Developing Your Optimal Level Of Arousal.

17

AT NIGHT UNDER THE LIGHTS
Acclimate
- Practice under the lights if you can to get used to the atmosphere, environment, shadows, and effects of lighting.
- Hit several more lobs and overheads than normal. This further accustoms your eyes to the light-to-dark-to-light flight of the balls.

PLAYING INDOORS
Roof Overhead
- Your indoor weather will be perfect. But make note of your ceiling clearance (it may be low).
- Hit more lobs in your warm up to practice keeping within the level of the ceiling.
- Hit a few more overheads in your warm up to get used to seeing a ceiling.

Crowds
- It will probably be crowded at the facility. Find a spot where you can feel comfortable.

Noise
- Prepare yourself mentally for the higher noise level of an enclosed and crowded building.

Inconvenience
- The facilities may be limited, so make the most of the essentials you pack in your bag.

Delay
- Delays are more common indoors. Expect and plan to manage your delays in a routine fashion which relaxes you and then restores your concentration for your match.

Prepare mentally as well as physically for adverse conditions.

PERSONAL NOTES

_____

_____

_____

_____

_____

_____

_____

_____

_____

_____

_____

_____

_____

_____

_____

_____

_____

_____

_____

_____

_____

_____

_____

ADVERSE CONDITIONS ARE A GREAT EQUALIZER!

DEALING WITH DISPUTES

On court disputes can distract you from your game. A dispute can take time to resolve, and it may be difficult for you to concentrate. The on court climate can become one of distress and distrust, challenging you emotionally. Here are three of the most common disputes and what I recommend in each situation. Try to resolve the conflict in a *quick, unemotional* fashion.

LINE CALLS

Have you ever been in the heat of a match, competing fiercely, only to get a bad line call at a crucial point, and you totally lost your mind? I know I have. The next time this happens, and you want to cross the net and wring this player's neck, try a strategy I call

Three Strikes, and You're Out!

THE FIRST STRIKE

My opponent has just made (what I believe) is a bad line call.

What You Do First
   Calmly walk up to the net. Ask politely, yet sternly, "Are you 100% sure that ball was out?"

One Possible Response
   This may do the trick. The other player may change his call. The player may realize that his clarity about where that ball hit was NOT 100%. You have given your opponent, who was not using his best judgement at the time of the call, a way out.

20

The Other Possible Response
Your opponent may stick to the call. Say to yourself,

"Strike One"

Continue playing as if nothing happened. Cue: Be calm and keep your focus on the match.

STRIKE TWO

It Happened Again!

What You Do Now
Again walk calmly to the net and ask as before, "Are you 100% sure that ball was out?" Reasoning may help at this point. If it was a crucial point, you might say, "I know this was a big point, and the ball WAS close. Are you sure that it was out?" Use this kind of language also on a first strike if the point is critical.

Response
If the 'striking' player changes his call...great! If not, say to yourself,

"Strike Two"

Continue playing as if nothing happened. Cue: Be calm and keep your focus on the match.

THE THIRD STRIKE

This Is The Third Time! Now I'm Getting Angry!

What You Do *Now*
Take a deep breath and count to 5 as you slowly exhale to release your anger. Walk calmly to the net and repeat as for Strike Two.

It is important that you do not antagonize your opponent at this time.

By now the 'striking' player will understand that you are upset. Becoming a bully will not be effective.

Rise above the situation and act with class. Whether the opponent changes the call now or not

"Strike Three!"

Put your racquet down. Let your opponent know your intention, and go to the tournament desk. Request a linesperson. Stay calm, and focus on resolving the problem rather than complaining about or reliving the past. When you get your linesperson, pay no attention to the existence of this official on the court.

Concentrate on your play!

LINESPERSON PRESENT

If you are in a dispute on a line call, you may approach the linesperson and politely ask, "How did you see that ball?" Regardless of the outcome, continue to play as if nothing has happened.

Special Note
> Be careful how often you go to the linesperson. If you are not getting overrules on what you think are bad calls, the linesperson may be getting irritated with your frequency of questioning calls.

LINE CALL DISPUTE HITLIST
- Stay calm and in the present. Forget the past.
- Breathe to release your anger and act with class.
- Avoid antagonizing your opponent.
- Request a linesperson at the third strike.
- *Remain focused on your game.*

Note
> If you allow bad calls, you allow yourself an excuse for losing. Take responsibility for your play and your actions. Get help when you need it. Let go of

your distress and other negative emotions. If you allow yourself to react by losing your 'cool,' you throw the advantage to your opponent.

BLATANT BAD CALLS

When you know you have received any blatant bad call (six inches or more within the court,) go directly to request a linesperson.

DISPUTE ON THE SCORE

Situation
>My opponent and I continue to have a problem agreeing on the score. What should I do?

Solution
>Call out the score after each point (in point of fact, this is the server's responsibility). Confirm the score after each point with your opponent.

SECOND BOUNCE

Situation
>Whose responsibility is it to call a second bounce on a shot?

Solution
>The person hitting the shot in question has the responsibility for calling "Second Bounce" on a shot. If you think it is, and your opponent does not call it, finish the point. Afterward, ask about the second bounce.

DEVELOPING YOUR OPTIMAL LEVEL OF AROUSAL

Optimal arousal is the level at which you best perform. The optimal level of arousal for you may be higher or lower than for someone else. Learn what performance level works best for you by observing yourself, by becoming self aware. Then, learn to control it. You can put yourself at your most effective competition level at the moment you need it by creating habits of behavior which get you there.

SELF AWARENESS
Tune Into Your Body
- Ask "What is going on for me, right now?" (physically and mentally.)
- Identify your own signs of under and over arousal.
- Decide whether your poorer performances are related to you being under-aroused or over-aroused.
- Compare what you do, how you prepare, mentally, for competitions you do well in, to your behavior prior to those competitions in which your performance was 'off.'

CONTROL
Develop Routines
- You want to have routines by which you handle particular situations. For instance, what do you think about when you are serving and the score is 5-2? And what, when the score is 3-4? And what do you think about when you are playing in high wind?
- Design your routines to work especially for you.

24

- Stick with your predetermined routine, both before and after the match, and in those situations for which you have a planned response.

PERSONAL NOTES

_____

_____

_____

_____

_____

_____

_____

_____

_____

_____

_____

_____

_____

_____

_____

_____

_____

_____

_____

_____

FIND YOUR IDEAL STATE AND STAY THERE!

Your level of physical and mental arousal will positively or negatively affect your performance on the court. With practice, you can *create your ideal arousal state* almost every time you step onto the court.

Learn to identify when you are under-aroused or over-aroused. Master methods to pump yourself up or bring yourself down.

UNDER AROUSAL
- You lack energy or 'fire'.
- You lack motivation (you feel bored, lazy).
- You experience feelings of helplessness.
- You have a depleted sense of anticipation or timing.
- Your threshold of patience is low.
- You experience that "I don't really care" feeling.
- You exhibit a noticeable absence of enthusiasm.
- You feel slow to start, like a 'cold engine.'

STRATEGIES TO BRING YOURSELF UP

Take Quick Short Breaths
    Forced, rapid breathing will increase your heart rate.

Bounce On Your Toes
    Jump up and down on your toes between points, before serving and returning. Get your body moving as often as possible.

Stimulate Your Imagination And Cue Yourself
    Think challenging ideas and thoughts. Use positive

statements or 'cue' words that trigger your sense of enthusiasm and excitement. Some examples might be: "Go for it!", and "Fight!"

Be Mindful Of Your Objectives
Mentally review your most important goals. Appeal to that enthusiastic person within you.

Have A Powerful Self Image
Create the strongest mental image you can of yourself playing in your finest hour, and recapture that *feeling*.

OVER AROUSAL
- You have an accelerated heartbeat.
- You exhibit darting eye movements.
- You feel or express emotional tension (nervousness).
- You experience increased muscle tension.
- You find yourself over-hitting your shots.
- You are too easily excited or frustrated.
- Your palms are sweaty.

STRATEGIES TO BRING YOURSELF DOWN
Breathe Deeply
Take slow rhythmic breaths, in through your nose and out through your mouth, breathing from your diaphragm.

Expend Energy
Hit a few minutes against a backboard to get rid of the 'jitters.' A light jog can also help you release some of your energy.

Relax
    Find a quiet place to sit and relax for a few minutes.
    Focus on your breathing. Contract and relax your
    muscles.

Maintain Your Perspective
    Accept the circumstances surrounding this match.
    Use your energy constructively by reviewing your
    strategy. Focus on how to manage the concerns that
    stress you.

Cue Yourself
    Use positive statements or 'cue' words that trigger a
    calm, relaxed, yet alert state of mind, such as, "Relax,"
    and "Stay cool."

Use Your Imagination
    Go somewhere in your mind that will put you in a
    more relaxed state. I like to go to the beach. Where
    do you go? Do this only on changeovers.

PERSONAL NOTES

_____

_____

_____

_____

_____

_____

_____

_____

_____

_____

_____

_____

_____

_____

_____

_____

_____

_____

_____

_____

KNOW YOUR SIGNS AND GET TO YOUR IDEAL STATE!

PLAYING WITHIN YOUR LIMITS

Are you about to face an opponent that you think is better that you? We have all been there, but do not worry. You can make the best of this situation, and maybe pull off an upset. This is a checklist for when you *think* you are in over your head.

SCOUT YOUR OPPONENT
- Watch this player in action, if possible, before your match.
- Look for something in the style of play which you might work to your advantage. See Scouting Your Opponent.
- Identify strengths and weaknesses you see.

GET INFORMATION
- Find out about this player from someone who is familiar with his or her style of play.

FORMULATE YOUR GAME PLAN
- See the section for Creating A Game Plan.

STAY FOCUSED
- Remember that any adverse condition can be an equalizer.
- Focus yourself mentally and emotionally on the task at hand.
- Be ready for any opportunity to gain an advantage.

LEARN FROM YOUR EXPERIENCE
- Playing better opponents can serve as a gauge to your progress, so play within your game to see how and where you are improving.

REMEMBER WHERE THE PRESSURE IS
- The pressure is *on your opponent* to win.
- You have nothing to lose.

PLAY THE PERCENTAGES
- You may not have to play above yourself to win, so compete with good percentage play.

JUST HAVE FUN
- Remember to enjoy just playing your best.
- Smile! Smiling is a good tension releaser.

Keep a positive attitude and give 100% effort.

PERSONAL NOTES

_____

_____

_____

_____

_____

_____

_____

_____

_____

_____

_____

_____

_____

_____

_____

_____

_____

_____

_____

_____

PLAY GOOD PERCENTAGE TENNIS!

PLAYING UP TO YOUR POTENTIAL

Playing an opponent a level below you can be challenging. This level player is often the toughest to compete well against. You may find it difficult to "psych up" against a player you know you are *supposed to defeat*. You do not appear to have anything to gain by competing against this type of opposition, *but you do!* These are some guidelines to assist you in your preparation for a lower level player.

SCOUT YOUR OPPONENT
- Watch this player in action, if possible, before your match.
- Look for something in the style of play which you might capitalize on to gain an advantage. See Scouting Your Opponent.
- Identify strengths and weaknesses you see.

GET INFORMATION
- Find out about this player for someone who is familiar with his or her style of play.

FORMULATE YOUR GAME PLAN
- See the section for Creating A Game Plan.

GET YOURSELF PSYCHED
- This is no time to relax. Get ready and maintain your usual routine. Refer to Managing Arousal Levels.

PLAY TO WIN!
- Be the consummate warrior. Show no mercy! You own this match, so play like it and act like it!

PLAY ONE POINT AT A TIME

- Your concentration may tend to waiver against this type of opponent. You can not afford to let up. Keep your focus on the job at hand.

Maintain a solid level of concentration.

PERSONAL NOTES

_____

_____

_____

_____

_____

_____

_____

_____

_____

_____

_____

_____

_____

_____

_____

_____

_____

_____

_____

_____

GET PSYCHED AND STAY FOCUSED!

CLOSING OUT A MATCH

When you are in a position to win your match, the steps you take to "close it out" are tremendously important.

Many players too easily fall victim to the pressures of this situation. Your concentration can waiver, your fears may dictate your decisions, and your muscles may tighten up. To maintain or achieve feelings of confidence and control in your match, do the following.

STICK WITH YOUR GAME PLAN
- Stay true to your *strategy*.
- Play the percentages and *focus on your performance*.

PLAY ONE POINT AT A TIME
- Maintain your concentration, and plan how you want your points to go for you: visualize it in your head. *Pay attention to each point*.

ATTEND TO DETAIL
- *Play the entire Point!* Expect your opponent to rise to the occasion and return every ball.

PLAY TO WIN
- Avoid 'playing not to lose.' This match is yours, so get out there and take it!

CONTROL YOUR TEMPO
- Be aware of maintaining your *tempo*. Stay in your rhythm and routine. Avoid the tendency to step up

your pace between points, becoming anxious to get to the end of a match.

REMEMBER TO BREATHE BETWEEN POINTS
- Balance your breathing by taking slow, deep, even breaths to remain calm and alert.

PLAN YOUR POINTS
- *Be deliberate* in executing your game plan. Following your game plan will keep you focused on what you have to do.

The pressure is on your opponent.

PERSONAL NOTES

_____

_____

_____

_____

_____

_____

_____

_____

_____

_____

_____

_____

_____

_____

_____

_____

_____

_____

_____

_____

_____

PLAN YOUR POINTS!

STAGING A COMEBACK

Okay, so you have just lost the first set. Or you may be starting the third set, after losing the second. Perhaps you are 'down BIG' in a particular set. Given any situation like these, one thing is for sure, *it's time for a change!*

I want you to consider the following before staging your comeback.

YOUR CURRENT GAME PLAN
- Is it a faulty game plan?
- Is it poor execution of a good game plan?
- Decide what adjustments you need to make, and get to it.

THE TEMPO
- Who is controlling the tempo between points and games?
- Can you break your opponent's momentum by changing the tempo?
- Within your comfort level, you might slow down or speed things up a bit.

YOUR COMPETITIVE DESIRE
- How hard are you willing to compete and *fight* to create this comeback?
- What has your arousal state been up to this point? Are you playing too low or too high?
  Use your arousal management skills to fire yourself up or bring yourself down to get ready for this comeback.

- Visualize this comeback in your head. *See it happen.*

PLAY IN THE PRESENT
- Learn from what has happened and move forward with your plan.
- Focus your attention on what you must do *now.*

Now that you have reevaluated and you have your plan for this comeback, *get back out there and make it happen!*

PERSONAL NOTES

_____

_____

_____

_____

_____

_____

_____

_____

_____

_____

_____

_____

_____

_____

_____

_____

_____

_____

_____

_____

NEVER SAY DIE!

MANAGING NEGATIVE EMOTIONS

Anger, fear and frustration usually divert your attention from the task at hand, and can destroy your confidence. The psychological stress you experience when you are resisting reality by giving in to these emotions cripples your ability to manage what you cannot change.

Sometimes negative emotions can be a good thing. Your anger, for instance, shows that you care about your performance. If you are under-psyched, you can use anger to pump yourself up. Yet, most of the time, your anger distracts you from concentrating on *what you have to do*.

Learning to simply be *aware* of your emotional state is the first step in redirecting your emotional energy. I strongly urge you to work toward mastering these methods for releasing, controlling, and redirecting your negative energy.

RELEASING BREATHS
- Take several slow, diaphragmatic breaths to release tension. This means you breathe from deep into your lower 'belly' or diaphragm.
- Breathe in through your nose and out through your mouth.
- Slowly count 5 as you breathe in and count 8 as you breathe out.
- Imagine negative energy leaving your body as you exhale.

VISUALIZATION

- Between points and changeovers, visualize yourself giving the performance that you want, consistent with your game plan.
- Focus on your performance, on what you need *to do* in order to win this match.

WALK THE WALK

- Act completely confident. Keep your head up and your chest out.
- The less your opponent knows about your emotional state, the better.

BE REALISTIC AND REMAIN IN THE PRESENT

- Accept each situation. Go point by point.
- Save your energy for the things you can change. This means **no emotional outbursts**.

STAY POSITIVE

- Take control of yourself by replacing each of your negative thoughts with a positive one.

BE OBJECTIVE

- The outcome of the match does not reflect who you are.
- Do not take points or matches personally.

ENJOY THE PROCESS

- Laugh at yourself. It is not life or death.
- Think of the game of tennis as an adventure, a series of journeys. Relax and enjoy the process.

Practice these techniques both on and off the court. Find which ones work best for you.

Everyone has negative feelings at one time or another. It is how you deal with this energy that can make or break you in competition and in your life.

Proper management of your emotions can greatly enhance your performance and enjoyment of the game.

PERSONAL NOTES

_____

_____

_____

_____

_____

_____

_____

_____

_____

_____

_____

_____

_____

_____

_____

_____

_____

_____

_____

_____

_____

REDIRECT YOUR ENERGY TO WORK FOR YOU!

FIGHTING THE CHOKING RESPONSE

You are in the heat of battle. Perhaps you are ready to serve out a set, or have a chance to break serve at 3-all. Or maybe you are in the middle of a tiebreaker. All of a sudden, your mind and body start to short circuit. Your palms are sweating, your heart is pounding, and your feet feel like lead. Fear sets in. You depart from your game plan, you begin to question your shot selection, and your unforced errors multiply. Before you know it, the match that should have been yours is lost. Sound familiar?

This is the fine art of Choking: giving in to fear, nervousness, and indecision. It appears to come out of nowhere, sudden and crippling. Fear is the enemy when choking, your fear of winning or losing. You choke when you allow your attention to move from what you have to do, your performance, to focus instead on the outcome of the match. The winning is in the DOING, not in the expectation of a result.

You do not have to fold under pressure. You can take steps to combat the enemy.

STEPS TO CONQUER CHOKING

Control Your Tempo

> You are likely to speed up your tempo between points when you are 'feeling the pressure.' Pay attention to your between point time and slow down if you need to.

Breathe!
Take slow, deep breaths. Exhale even longer than you inhale. It is not possible to be in fear when you breathe from your diaphragm. Fearful breathing is short and located in your upper chest.

Plan Your Points
Focus on the 'now' and on your performance. Think about specific strategy. Be decisive.

- Where should I serve? *I will slice the ball into his body.*
- Should I come to the net or stay back? *I am going to keep the ball deep to her backhand until I get a short ball I can pounce on.*

Stick To Your Game Plan
If it has been working for you, then stick with it. Critical places in the match are not the time to try something new.

Keep Moving
Bounce up and down on your toes to keep your blood circulating and your feet activated.

Lighten Up
Smile. Give your opponent something to think about: throw a smile his way. Relax and have fun. Your value as a person does not depend on the outcome of this match.

CLOSING IN ON YOUR OPPONENT

You are now calm, yet alert and confident. You have a plan for 'now.' You are doing battle with your opponent instead of yourself. It is up to your opponent to take this match away from you. If he or she rises to the occasion, so be it. You continue to focus on yourself, on your performance, and on taking control of the situation.

Good Luck!

PERSONAL NOTES

_____
_____
_____
_____
_____
_____
_____
_____
_____
_____
_____
_____
_____
_____
_____
_____
_____
_____
_____
_____
_____
_____

SMILE AND FOCUS ON YOUR PERFORMANCE!

FUELING YOURSELF FOR COMPETITION

How you refuel your body before your next match can enhance your performance or detract from it. Choose the kinds of foods that will quickly gain and sustain your energy. You want your meal to keep you alert and ready to compete, NOW!

COMPLEX CARBOHYDRATES: Whole Grains
Fruits And Vegetables

Complex carbohydrates are 'energy foods.' Carbohydrates are stored in the body in the form of glycogen. When you exercise, your body breaks down glycogen to glucose. Glucose fuels your exercising muscles. When your glycogen is depleted, you become exhausted.

Any pre-competition meal or snack should consist mostly of complex carbohydrates to quickly replace your stores of glycogen. While fats and protein will eventually give you energy, you do not have the hours it takes today. Here are your guidelines.

AVOID OVEREATING OR RUSHED EATING
- The size of your meal depends on your time schedule. The general rule is to consume approximately 100 calories (25 grams of carbohydrates) per hour before your competition. Find out the carbohydrate content of your meal beforehand, if possible.
- Chew well and eat in a quiet place to assist your digestion.

50

AVOID FATS, PROTEIN, CAFFEINE, AND SUGAR
- Make competition meals 60% to 80% complex carbohydrates.
- Choose whole grains: breads, pasta, cereals, ricecakes, etc.
- Stay away from sugar. It may get you 'up' for a short time, but your energy level will fall quickly.
- Avoid caffeine as it contributes to the dehydration of the body.
- Choose fruits and vegetables.

DRINK PLENTY OF WATER
- Drink more water than your thirst tells you to drink.
- Drink a 6 to 8 oz. glass of water before or with your meal for every 50 pounds of body weight. Don't wait to be dehydrated.

PACK FUEL SNACKS
- Pack easily carried 'carbs' you can snack on, especially for competitions. (Examples are fruit, sports bars, fruit juice, and bagels.) You may not get time to go out to eat between matches.
- Although sports bars are easy to carry in your bag and are fairly high in 'carbs', they are also high in fiber, which absorbs quite a bit of water from your body. So consume 12 - 16 ounces of water with your energy bar.

Be sure of your energy by eating smart.

PERSONAL NOTES

_____
_____
_____
_____
_____
_____
_____
_____
_____
_____
_____
_____
_____
_____
_____
_____
_____
_____
_____
_____

GET THE PROPER FUEL FOR YOUR MATCH!

BASIC SPORTS MEDICINE

My wish is for you to remain physically sound for optimal play. And while we all have aches and pains on the court, facing challenges with the environment or soft tissue soreness, this section will help you act when you know something is wrong. I include physical and mental warm-up guidelines for avoiding problems. I strongly advise you to give yourself a full ounce of prevention at all times.

THE ENVIRONMENT: HEAT

Playing in the heat can be dangerous. Practice extreme caution and awareness to prevent over-heating your body. Here are the two most common conditions.

Muscle Cramps
- Muscle cramps are most commonly caused by a depletion of water or an electrolyte imbalance in the body.
- The severity of the pain will dictate how much longer you can play.

Heat Exhaustion
- This condition occurs when the thermoregulatory system, the 'cooling' system, of the body slows down. The symptoms are:

nausea	dizziness
stomach ache	profuse sweating
headache	shortness of breath
vomiting	skin–cool to the touch

As a basic rule of thumb, if you exhibit three or more of these symptoms, you probably have some form of heat exhaustion.

Basic Treatment for Heat Exhaustion
- Cease the activity.
- Replace water and electrolytes orally at a moderate speed.
- Drink water or mix it 1:1 with a sports drink.
- Create mild body cooling. Get into the shade, loosen your clothing, fan yourself, apply cool water to your neck and wrists.
- Massage cramps mildly.

Blistering
The two most common places you will blister are on your hands and feet. In either case, once the blister becomes too painful here is what you can do.

- Clean the area with soap and water or prepacked moistened towelettes.
- Drain the blister with a sterilized needle if it has not yet broken.
- Dry the area with something clean and protect it with a bandage.

If you have more time, hold off on the bandage and apply a layer or two of an antiseptic 'liquid bandage' (available at most drug stores). Let the area air dry completely. If the blister is on your foot, you can put on a dry pair of socks to reduce your foot to shoe friction.

SOFT TISSUE INJURIES
Dealing with strains and sprains can be annoying and tedious. Nevertheless, with proper rest and continued treatment to the injury, you can recover completely in

a matter of days. This is an acronym of the basics for initial treatment of strains and sprains.

P - protect
R - rest
I - ice
C - compress
E - elevation (above your head if possible)

These treatments are generally recommended to help reduce the swelling in order for an expert to evaluate the injury properly. See an orthopedic physician as soon as possible.

An Ice Treatment
- Treat the area with ice for twenty minutes at a time.
- Use a cold pack or bag of ice (do not use a towel).
- Elevate the injured area above the level of your heart, if possible.
- You can ice the area several times a day.
- Wait at least 30 minutes between treatments.
- You can massage the area with ice for the same period of time.
- For ice massage, freeze water in a paper cup (remove the cup).

Anti-Inflammatory
- An anti-inflammatory such as ibuprofen can be taken orally.
- Follow the directions on the label of the bottle.

Treating injury as recommended here will prepare you for but does not replace diagnosis and treatment by a qualified physician.

THE PROPER WARM-UP

To help prevent soft tissue injuries and to relax yourself before a match, practice a good warm-up routine. This will increase your range of motion, and help get your heart rate and breathing pace up to what a match requires. Here are basic guidelines for warming-up.

Develop A Routine Warm-Up
- Develop a warm-up you know well and can repeat methodically.
- Repeat your warm-up ROUTINE just before your pre-match and actual match hitting warm-up on court.

Elevate Tissue Temperature
- Do some light jogging, jumping rope, or calisthenics.
- You know your body is warm enough when you break a sweat.

Static Stretching
- Isolate the muscle groups. I recommend you follow the USTA Basic 10, as a visual guide.
- Hold the muscle group for a solid 15 to 20 seconds. Maintain even breathing.
- Avoid ballistic stretching (bouncing) which can encourage or actually cause injury.

Dynamic Stretching
- Perform fluid movements, stretching more than one muscle group.
- Examples: shadow stroking, arm circles.

Quick Check On Court
- Check your body for areas that may still be tight.
- Perform further stretches to loosen and warm tight or sore spots.
- You are now ready to hit balls.

STAY WARM

If you are going to hit balls before your match, it is important to keep your body temperature up between the time you finish hitting and your match time.

With a proper warm-up you will be *more relaxed and loose,* a terrific competitive edge as well as a protection from harm.

This practice can save you weeks of discomfort from injury.

MENTAL WARM-UP

A mental warm-up puts you in the present. It is important to align your mental and physical presence for your match. You can better avoid injury from carelessness when your body and your match have your full attention.

A mental warm-up means you determine a clear course of action for your day. You want to:

- Turn your attention to the place of practice or competition. Focus on your plan.

- Visualize yourself executing good plays during your stretching. This will aid in your focus on your match and add to your confidence, similar to a dress rehearsal for a play.

- Leave all other cares and concerns at the door as you head out for your match or practice.

You will now have your focus and energy concentrated on each specific tennis activity and challenge you meet.

PERSONAL NOTES

_____

_____

_____

_____

_____

_____

_____

_____

_____

_____

_____

_____

_____

_____

_____

_____

_____

_____

_____

_____

_____

_____

TAKE CARE OF YOUR INJURIES!

WINNING ATTITUDES FOR MENTAL TOUGHNESS

As you excel in your physical skills, gaining mental toughness becomes a higher priority for your continued improvement.

I define mental toughness as *being in total control of the moment.*

Sports psychologists agree that your attitude about pursuing mental toughness is critical to your development as a player. I have consolidated my research for you into four winning attitudes.

MAKE A COMMITMENT

First and foremost, you must make a definite commitment to becoming mentally tough. By making this decision, you fuel your motivation to develop all of your talent.

TAKE RESPONSIBILITY

Take responsibility for everything you control. Accept your actions, good and bad, and gain control of your thoughts. Take charge!

THRIVE ON ADVERSITY

Adversity is everywhere. Instead of spending your energy trying to avoid the inescapable, thrive on it, be inspired by it, let it challenge you to be your best. Work adversity to your advantage.

MAKE TENNIS FUN

Learn to enjoy the battle, the struggle, the journey. Tennis invites you to many great adventures. By enjoying the process, you will grow to be a great competitor.

Pursuing and improving your mental toughness will greatly enhance your performance as a player. It is the one limitless aspect of the game over which you may exert total control.

CREATING YOUR
TRAINING PROGRAM

A training program is the map by which you find your way from where you are now, physically and mentally, to where you want to be: that which you wish to become.

Shape your program around your calendar of competition. Make it comprehensive yet simple. Consider what your wish to achieve in your fitness and agility, playing status, physical skills, mental toughness, and overall health and wellness. Schedule practices and events which move you toward your goals.

Training represents a gradually increasing demand on you and your body which develops your game. Your body will respond naturally to the demands you make on it. How you improve and how much you enjoy the game directly relates to the development of your program.

GUIDELINES TO CREATING YOUR TRAINING PROGRAM
Identify Your Seasons
- Define your competitive season and your off season.
- Even if you play every week of the year, decide which part of the year is the most important and which part is more developmental.
- Taper your program in order to peak at certain important events.

Decide When You Will Train
- Set up a program you can sustain throughout the season.
- Decide how many hours you will commit to tennis each day, and how many days each week.
- To be workable, your approach to training must be realistic. Make the program practical, convenient, accessible, and enjoyable, to avoid overstressing yourself.

Set Goals
- Identify your strengths and weaknesses; earmark areas you most need to improve.
- Set challenging yet attainable goals. Be specific and orient your goals toward your performance.

I want to develop a serve and volley game.
I want to become a quicker player on the court.
I want to improve directional control with my second serve.

- Set both long and short term goals. Work on changes in the off-season or the developmental part of the year.

Make Your Program Dynamic
- You can incorporate cross-training. For example: play basketball, soccer, etcetera, for footwork and fitness workouts.
- A varied program helps you stay fresh and avoid burn out.

Consult A Professional
- A USPTA or USPTR professional can give you substantial help in designing a program which meets your needs and desires.

DURING YOUR TRAINING YEAR

Listen To Your Body
Stay aware of when to push yourself and when it is better to back off. Be flexible with yourself.

Laugh Often
Have some fun out there! Tennis should be a delight to pursue, not a tribulation. Humor is a healthy sign that you are maintaining a balanced perspective of yourself in relation to your competition.

Be Patient
Realize that progress is mechanical: some areas will improve more gradually than others. Believe that whatever you practice over time, with attention and commitment toward improvement, will eventually establish you where you want to be.

Educate Yourself
Read about the game, about competition. Read about self-mastery, about health and fitness. Find new aspects of improvement you can incorporate into your training program. To grow as a player, develop your own knowledge base.

Have A Dream
Your dream can be an outcome such as achieving a particular ranking or winning a certain tournament. Your dream gives you direction.

SUGGESTED READING

Intelligent Tennis, A Sensible Approach to Playing Your Best Tennis...Consistently, by Skip Singleton, Betterway Publications, Inc., 1988.

Mental Toughness Training For Sports, Achieving Athletic Excellence, by Jim Loehr, Ed D., The Stephen Green Press, 1982.

New Toughness Training For Sports, by James E. Loehr, Penguin Books, 1994.

No Ordinary Moments, A Peaceful Warrior's Guide To Daily Life, by Dan Millman, H.J. Kramer, Inc., 1992

Power Tennis Training, by Donald A. Chu, PhD., Human Kinetics, 1995.

Sports Nutrition Guidebook, Nancy Clark, MS, RD, Leisure Press, Champaign, IL, 1990.

Stretching, by Bob Anderson, Shelter Publications, Inc., 1980.

The Inner Athlete, by Dan Millman, Stillpoint Publishing, 1994.

The Inner Game of Tennis, by Tim Gallway, Random House, 1974.

The Mental Advantage, Developing Your Psychological Skills in Tennis, by Robert S. Weinberg, PhD., Leisure Press, A Division of Human Kinetics Publishers, 1988.

The Mental Game, Winning at Pressure Tennis, by James E. Loehr, Plume, A Division of Penguin Books, 1990.

The Science of Coaching Tennis, by Jack L. Groppel, PhD., with Loehr, Mellville, and Quinn, Leisure Press, 1989.

<u>Thinking Body, Dancing Mind</u>, by Chungliang Al Huang, and Jerry Lynch, Bantam Books, 1992.

<u>Total Tennis Training</u>, by Chuck Kriese, Masters Press, 1988.

<u>Tournament Tough</u>, by Carlos Goffi, Holt, Rinehart & Winston, 1984.

Intelligent Tennis, A Sensible Approach to Playing Your Best Tennis...Consistently, by Skip Singleton, Betterway Publications, Inc., 1988.

Mental Toughness Training For Sports, Achieving Athletic Excellence, by Jim Loehr, Ed D., The Stephen Green Press, Lexington, Massachusetts, copyright 1982.

The Inner Athlete, by Dan Millman, Stillpoint Publishing, Walpole, New Hampshire, copyright 1994.

The Mental Advantage, Developing Your Psychological Skills in Tennis, by Robert S. Weinberg, PhD., Leisure Press, A Division of Human Kinetics Publishers, 1988.

USEFUL CONTACTS:

United States Tennis Association   (212) 302-3322

For more information concerning LGE Tennis Programs and Products:

LGE Sport Science, Inc.
9803 Lake Nona Road
Orlando, Florida 32827   (800) 543-7764
                                (407) 438-9911
                                (407) 438-6667 facsimile

ORDER FORM

If you would like to place an order for **The Player's Hitlist,** you may do so below. Call 1-800-770-0892 for the wholesale price breakdown. Good luck on your journey!

Book	**Price**	**Quantity**	**Subtotal**
The Player's Hitlist	9.95		

Subtotal	_____
San Antonio residents add 8.25% sales tax, other Texas residents add 7.25% sales tax	_____
Shipping & Handling*	_____
Total	_____

* Shipping & Handling charges:
1) Contiguous 48 United States: $5 first lb. plus $.50 each additional lb.
2) Alaska, Hawaii, Puerto Rico and Canada: $10 2nd day air or $15 next day air.
3) Other countries: $20 first lb. plus $6 each additional lb.

Please make check payable and send orders to:
Essential Sports Products
P.O. Box 15451
San Antonio, Texas 78212